THE MEMOIRS OF NAIM BEY

Turkish Official Documents
relating to the Deportations and
Massacres of Armenians

COMPILED

BY

ARAM ANDONIAN

THE MEMOIRS OF NAIM BEY

Turkish Official Documents
relating to the Deportations and
Massacres of Armenians

COMPILED

BY

ARAM ANDONIAN

With an introduction by Viscount Gladstone

reprinted by

Suzeteo Enterprises

The Memoirs of Naim Bey: Turkish Official Documents Relating to the Deportations and Massacres of Armenians

Compiled by Aram Andonian
Introduction by Viscount Gladstone

ISBN: 978-1-947844-69-8

A word from the Publisher:

The Memoirs of Naim Bey was originally published in 1920, making it in the public domain. In 1964, the Armenian Historical Research Association reprinted a facsimile of the book. This present edition is based on that facsimile.

This present edition is *not* a facsimile. It has carefully re-constructed the original text *from* a facsimile. In doing so has incorporated the corrections listed on the 'errata' page inserted along with the 1964 reprint of the facsimile. Wherever these corrections were made, a note has been made in the footnotes, along with the original 1920 text. No attempt was made to ascertain whether or not the items listed on the 'errata' were in fact accurate.

Apart from these changes, and the footnotes, the text is intended to be exactly as Aram Andonian first wrote it.

In this edition, the photos which Aram Andonian had interspersed throughout his text have all been moved to the end.

At the end of the text are 26 photos which the Armenian Historical Research Association appended to their facsimile edition. A good faith assessment of those photos suggests that all of these photos are also in the public domain. They are included in this text because of their powerful testimony to the fate of countless Armenians.

There is some controversy within academic circles about whether or not the documentation provided by Naim Bey, as compiled by Aram Andonian, are accurate. The Publisher takes no position on this controversy and has endeavored only to faithfully reproduce the original, so that scholars themselves can make their own determinations on the merits or demerits of the contents.

FOREWORD

The Author of the present work, Mr. Aram Andonian, is one of the Armenian intellectuals who were arrested and exiled from Constantinople on Saturday, April 11, 1915, without any trial and with no sentence except the decision of a committee.

Mr. Aram Andonian, who had been appointed Military Censor at the time of the mobilisation, was arrested in Constantinople on the accusation of having conveyed news of the murder of Sahag Vartabed, Bishop of Shabin Karahissar, and of the massacre at Skhert, to the Armenian Patriarchate. He had been betrayed by a Turkish official. The Military Tribunal at Constantinople had not been able to prove this accusation, but as the suspicion against him remained, he was dismissed from his post and sent to the Labour Battalion to do fatigue duty. He succeeded in escaping, but was arrested and driven with others to be sent to Diarbekir.

To be exiled to Diarbekir was equivalent to a death sentence, as it was an understood thing that those condemned to exile in that place were to be murdered before reaching their pretended destination, and any Turkish official, gendarme or policeman, in fact, any Mussulman, was free to do away with them at any suitable point. Among those murdered *en route* were three Armenian members of the Turkish Parliament—Zohrab, Vartkes and Dr. Daghavarian. When the real meaning of a sentence of banishment to Diarbekir became known, Mardin was substituted for Diarbekir, and then exiles to Mardin were murdered on the way.

On the way to Diarbekir, Mr. Andonian broke his leg, and they were obliged to cast him into a hospital, where he remained until the wholesale deportations began, when he was one of those that were driven to Der Zor. Then, after a series of escapes and re-arrests, he finally reached Aleppo, where he was again arrested, but was rescued by friends, who managed to obtain a permit for his temporary residence in the town.

INTRODUCTION

Search the blood-stained annals of the Ottoman Empire and nothing comparable to the atrocities of the past five years can be found. The awful story of the extermination of men, women and children by the direct order of the Turkish Government is beyond words. For cold and bestial cruelty the names of Enver and Talaat are consigned to undying infamy.

Readers of this significant Memoir must form, as I have done, their own conclusions.

We know the horrible facts. It is well to know also how and by whom the massacres were organised and perpetrated.

We are about to make a Treaty with the governing Turk reeking of deeds surpassing in magnitude and vileness the most imaginative pictures of hell ever conceived.

It is right to note that even their instruments sometimes showed pity and that some Turkish officials are good and humane men.

But for the Turkish Government the strongest words are ineffective. If there is anything in the modern conception of duty and justice, the Treaty that has yet to come must rescue once and for all the survivors of this Christian nation from the unutterable misdoings of the "Sublime Porte."

GLADSTONE.

December 24, 1919.

TRANSLATOR'S INTRODUCTION

The history of Armenia's martyrdom still lacks a great deal before its records are completed.

The victims could not even make their voices reach the civilised world, because they fell in far-away unknown corners, and uninhabited desert places; and it is only a few faint echoes of their dying agony and of their unspeakable sufferings that Lord Bryce through his sense of justice has succeeded in making heard. His records, unfortunately, only come down to 1916. But the most terrible crimes and the greatest massacres took place after 1916.

What is principally lacking in the records of Armenia's martyrdom is the voice of conscience on the part of the millions who constitute the nation that is entirely responsible for this fearful crime.

The Turks were intoxicated with the assurance of victory after the great defeat of Russia, and that intoxication justified the slaughter of the Armenians in their eyes; it constituted one more spray in the wreath of victory which they already imagined to be crowning their heads.

It is the voice of that conscience concerning the martyrdom that I am making heard in the present publication. It is a Turk who is going to speak through me— a Turk who was charged with the task of carrying out the policy of exterminating the whole Armenian nation, and through whose hands have passed all the official orders for the deportations and massacres.

That Turk, by name Naim Bey, is the late chief secretary of the Deportations Committee of Aleppo. This Committee was the principal organiser of the fearful deportations. When the Committee saw that there were great numbers of Armenian deportees in Meskene and all along the banks of the Euphrates, they sent Naim Bey to hasten matters. But Naim Bey was not the man for that work, because he was not a bad man. I had heard a good report of him, how he had actually helped some Armenian families to escape, taking nothing in return, in spite of the fact that his finances were not in a very brilliant condition. He might have demanded anything he liked from those families who were rich, and for whom being sent back to the desert would have certainly meant being condemned to death.

For two years and a half I had been pursued by persecution, living in hiding, now in Aleppo, now in Damascus and Beirout, and sometimes in the Lebanon, till the English entered Aleppo, bringing liberty with them. Some friends from Adana then reminded me of Naim Bey, and promised to facilitate the satisfaction of my great desire to see him. Considering his long term of office in the General Deportations Committee at Aleppo, it seemed to me that he ought to know a great deal—everything, in fact. "The departure of the Turks from Aleppo, after the arrival of the English, was something like the escape of criminals," he said to me. "I, having a clear conscience, did not wish to join them, and I stayed."

As the Government of the Young Turks has caused the documents concerning the massacre of Armenians to disappear, we had no official evidence to show. It was this want which Naim Bey supplied by handing over to us a great many official documents, ministerial telegrams and decrees to Governors sent on behalf of the Ittihad Committee, which had passed through his hands during his term of office under the General Deportations Committee of Aleppo, some of which he had kept, perhaps fearing future responsibility; one part of those documents he has written from memory, and the most important ones are photographed and published in the present work.

His whole statement took weeks to make. He would write it down bit by bit and bring it to me, because he was obsessed till the end with the terror that those papers which he brought me one by one would be detrimental to his race. Every time he would swear that what he brought was the last, and every time he condemned me to fresh and greater efforts. The work of persuading him became a torment which I gladly underwent.

After the arrival of the English I made all the surviving Armenian women, girls and men who could remember, write down their experiences, and it was easy for me to verify the memoirs of Naim Bey. These memoirs give a correct description of what happened, but they omit to mention many events and many people because of the indecision and interruptions which hampered Naim Bey while he was writing them.

Three great massacres took place after 1916.

Men, women and children from Constantinople and the surrounding district, from the Anatolian railway line and Cilicia, were driven into the desert, where they met people from the six Armenian provinces and from the shores of the Black Sea, but this latter contingent consisted only of women, girls and boys of seven or under, as every male over seven had been slaughtered. All these were the victims of the three massacres. The first massacre was that of Res-ul-Ain, in which 70,000 people were killed; the second took place at Intilli, where there were 50,000 people assembled, most of them working on a tunnel of the Baghdad Railway; and the third, which was the most fearful of all, at Der Zor, where Zia Bey slaughtered nearly 200,000 Armenians.

These figures only give the numbers of people killed by massacre. If we add to their numbers the victims of misery, sickness and hunger, especially in Res-ul- Ain and Der Zor, the number of Armenians who were slain or died in the desert will exceed a million.

The Memoirs of Naim Bey begin from the time of the preparations for the massacre in Res-ul-Ain. This place is a camp of Circassians established amongst the ruins of what was once the kingdom of Mesopotamia, and hardly numbers more than fifty houses, but, happening to be on the line of the Baghdad Railway, it suddenly grew to be of great importance.

THE MEMOIRS OF NAIM BEY

I BELIEVE that the history of the Armenian deportations and massacres, which have rendered the name of Turk worthy of eternal malediction on the part of all humanity, has no parallel in any record of inhuman deeds which has been written until this day. In whatever corner of the wide territories of Turkey one may look, whatever dark ravine one may investigate, thousands of Armenian corpses and skeletons will be found, slaughtered and mutilated in the most cruel manner.

I had as yet not had anything to do with the work of deportation. I was a secretary in the employment of the Tobacco Regie at Res-ul-Ain. I saw a caravan outside the village, by the riverside, composed of hundreds of miserable women and children. They used to come to the village every morning to beg. Some of them carried water, and tried to live on the crust of bread which they earned in that way.

It was summer as yet. They could shelter themselves in the clefts of some rock or mound, but, when the winter came, one could hear the moaning of those that were dying of cold and hunger all through the stillness of the long night. The Circassians of the village heard them too, but those dying moans touched neither their hearts nor their consciences.

I shall never forget that night. I was at the house of the Kaimakam; a storm was raging outside; within ten minutes' walk from where we were we could hear the sobs and moans of those unhappy people outside, exposed to the fury of the elements. The Kaimakam, Yousouf Zia Bey, was a very good, kind-hearted man. We went out together to the house of an Agha, and to one or two other places, whence we managed to get hold of two or three tents. With the help of ten or fifteen gendarmes, and some of the people, we succeeded in pitching the tents, so that the poor victims might have some sort of shelter. Their death was a pitiful thing to behold; but an

1

infinitely more heart-rending scene took place when the dogs began to devour the corpses.

These were the remnants of the unhappy Armenian populations of Sivas, Diarbekir and Kharput. About one million inhabitants were being transplanted from five or six provinces. By the time they arrived at the place of exile destined for them, there were hardly a hundred or, a hundred and fifty women and children left in each caravan, which meant that they were slaughtered as they were brought along.

I came to Aleppo. As luck would have it, Abdullahad Nouri Bey, who had arrived three or four days before as Representative of the General Deportations Committee, appointed me his Chief Secretary.

Although I had seen things with my own eyes while I was at Res-ul-Ain, I had not been able to understand the purpose of those crimes. I only grasped their nature and spirit afterwards. Every time I recorded the secret orders given in cipher documents I trembled. A great nation was sentenced to death with its women and babies.

First the Government decided that the deported Armenians should be driven to Maara, Bab, and other outlying districts of Aleppo, and then orders were given that "the destination of the Armenians is around the river Khabaur[1] (near Der Zor)."

One day the following telegram came from the Minister of the Interior—

> The purpose of sending away Certain People[2] is to safeguard the welfare of our fatherland for the future, for wherever they may live they will never abandon their seditious ideas, so we must try to reduce their numbers as much as possible.

---

[1] In the 1920 text, "Khan-Zor."

[2] In all the official communications regarding the deportations and massacres, as well as other kindred operations, the designation *"certain people"* is used for the Armenians.

This telegram arrived in November 1915. Eight days afterwards, without even being ratified by the Governor-General, it was given to Abdullahad Nouri Bey. The very same evening at 11.30 (Turkish time) the superintendent of the deportees, Eyoub Bey, and the head of the gendarmerie, Emin Bey, hurried to the Government offices to see Nouri Bey. Nouri Bey at once showed them the telegram he had received, and they were together for about an hour. The subject of their conversation was the method of exterminating the Armenians. Eyoub Bey was for openly exterminating them, but Abdullahad Nouri Bey, who was a very cunning man, disapproved of this plan. His idea was that it would be better to expose the Armenian deportees to want and to the rigour of the winter; killing them in this way would serve in the future as evidence to prove the story that they had died a natural death.

Till then the gendarmes had not interfered with affairs concerning deportees in Aleppo. But now the gendarmerie began to co-operate with the police.

Very soon great activity began in Aleppo. The deportees crowded into the districts of Gatma[3] and Kilis, and around Aleppo they were sent in companies to Akterim, and from there to Bab. And it turned out exactly as the officials had anticipated. Every day news reached us of hundreds of deaths, through hunger, cold and sickness.

Eyoub Bey went to Azaz. On his return he went in great glee to the seat of government. He told how he had burnt the tents. Bab was crowded. Typhus was making ravages everywhere. The Kaimakam and the officials charged with the work of deportation sent reports of deaths every day. Death did not only strike the Armenians; it slaughtered the native population as well.

One day I said to Abdullahad Nouri Bey: "Bey Effendi, let us relax the deportation of the Armenians a little, for in

---

[3] In the 1920 text, "Garma."

this way death is threatening the whole of Mesopotamia. None but devils will remain in those wide stretches of land. The Kaimakam of Res-ul-Ain is making painful communications about this."

Nouri Bey laughed.

"My boy," he said, "in this way we rid ourselves of two dangerous elements at once. Is it not the Arabs who are dying with the Armenians? Is it a bad thing? The road for Turkey's future will be cleared!"

I listened. This fearful answer made me tremble.

What was it that encouraged the man to continue so boldly and fearlessly in the execution of such a cruel and diabolical plan? Much might be said with to this. But the copy of an order which was found amongst the secret papers of the Deportations Committee is sufficient in itself to explain the fearlessness and daring with which Nouri Bey was carrying out the work entrusted to him—the work of completely exterminating the Armenians.

This is the order—

> Although the extermination of the Armenian element, which has for centuries been desirous of destroying the sure foundation of our Empire, and has now taken the form of a real danger, had been decided upon earlier than this, circumstances did not permit us to carry out this sacred intention. Now that all obstacles are removed, and the time has come for redeeming our fatherland from this dangerous element, it is urgently recommended that you should not be moved to feelings of pity on seeing their miserable plight; but, by putting an end to them all, try with all your might to obliterate the very name 'Armenia' from Turkey. See to it that those to whom you entrust the carrying out of this purpose are patriotic and reliable men.

The date of this order is not known, nor is it known to whom it was addressed, because it was a copy. Everything points, however, to its having been sent on behalf of Talaat Pasha, the Minister of the Interior, straight to the Governor-General, and having been forwarded by the Government to the Deportations Committee. This order must have reached Aleppo before the arrival of Abdullahad Nouri Bey, probably during the administration of Jelal Bey. Perhaps it was on the strength of this that Jelal Bey wired to Constantinople, saying, I am the Governor of this province; I cannot be its executioner." He was dismissed at once, and Beker Sami Bey, a man who was also opposed to the massacres, was sent to Aleppo in his place.

The General Supervisor of the deportees, Shukri Bey, had already been several months in Aleppo, and was organising the plan of the deportations and massacres. But he could not find people trustworthy enough to carry out the terrible project. The Governor-General, Jelal Bey, was not dismissed yet; it was impossible to get help from him. The Chief of the Police, Fikri Bey, was under the influence of Jelal Bey, and he also disapproved of the massacres, so there was no hope from him either. The only hope of Shukri Bey was Jemal Bey, who had been sent from Adana specially to superintend the Armenian massacres. The two were working together to put the fearful crime into effect, but they could not do anything.

Two Armenian brothers, Onik and Armenak Mazloumian, personal friends of Jelal Bey and Fikri Bey, were the greatest obstacles in the way of Shukri and Jemal, as they were trying to mitigate the evil, even if they could not prevent it altogether. Their hotel in Aleppo (Baron's Hotel), besides being an inn, was the place where one branch of the Government had its seat; in fact, it was almost a Government building, because the Governor, the Chief of the Police, and nearly all the officials used to meet there constantly. The position of these two Armenians was a strange one during all that terrible time. One of them, Onik Mazloumian, was incapable of cringing to any one; he did not know how to hold his tongue, and he could not pretend to be what he was not. It is difficult for such a straightforward and daring person to get on with the Turks. His nature was so lovable, he was so generous in spending all his wealth on entertaining the people who might any day become the executioners of his nation, that he succeeded in gaining a great influence, which he used in trying to save his compatriots.

On Thursday in Passion Week he was asked by Abdullahad Nouri Bey what brand of champagne he was going to bring out that Easter. "Our Easter," he replied, "will begin on the day of your departure."

The younger brother, Armenak, was also a man who did not know how to disguise or hide his feelings. He, too, treated all these officials with extravagant generosity, and even when a man with the evil reputation of Zeki Bey came to Aleppo on his way to Der Zor, he invited him to his house and tried to make him feel friendly towards the Armenians. He was at the Police Headquarters almost every day to intervene on behalf of some individual, or some family.

Jemal Pasha liked and protected the two brothers. Shukri Bey understood that they were an obstacle to him, and would call out—

First of all that nest (Baron's Hotel) should be cleared out.

It was after the appointment of Mustafa Abdullhalik Bey as Governor-General of Aleppo that those fearful massacres took place.

At first there was an Executive Committee in the Deportations Committee of Aleppo, by means of which the deportations of the Armenians to the desert were carried out. So long as the work was in the hands of this executive committee, the deportees were to a certain extent immune from spoliation and brutal treatment. The Government, realising that they could not effect their ultimate purpose in this way, dismissed the Governor (Bekir Sami Bey), and sent in his place Mustafa Abdullhalik Bey, who was already won over to their purpose. This man was an enemy of the Armenians, and tried, in the name of Turkey, to crush out the whole Armenian race. The orders sent by him to the Deportations Committee are so ruthless that one can hardly explain them. Some of the Armenian members of the Ottoman Parliament had—probably with many supplications—succeeded in obtaining from the Ministry of the Interior permission for their families to remain in Aleppo. The Ministry of the Interior sent orders about them to Mustafa Abdullhalik Bey, but he concealed these orders, and sent those families also away to the desert.

I know of fifteen or twenty families which had received permission to stay in Aleppo, but which he sent to the desert.

The Government had given Abdullahad Nouri Bey as a colleague to this man. The representative of the General Deportations Committee, Nouri Bey was a very clever and naturally cruel man, and he was filled with a special enmity against the Armenians. He was an incarnation of refinement of cruelty. The sufferings and misery of the Armenians, the frequent reports of deaths among them, filled him with such rapture that he almost danced with joy, because all these things were the result of his orders. "The Government does not want these people.to live,"he would say. He used to say that, when he was called to this office, as he was leaving for Aleppo, the Advisor of the Ministry of the Interior suggested that he should see Talaat Pasha before he left. Nouri Bey went to the Sublime Porte. There were a few guests with the Pasha.

"When do you leave?" he asked, then, rising, he took him to the window, and said in an undertone: "Of course you know what the work is that you are expected to do. I must see Turkey rid of those cursed people" (the Armenians).

Jemal Pasha had ordered that five or six Armenian families who had been working (with their carts) in the tunnel of

Intilli, should go to Damascus. The Governor had communicated this order to Nouri Bey, who added the following inscription to it—

Does a great Government, which has deported hundreds of thousands of Armenians, need two broken carts belonging to a handful of Armenians, that these people should be separated from the General Deportation to the desert, and sent to Damascus?

He was a very nervous and a very strict man.[4]

Abdullahad Nouri Bey's principal colleague was his immediate subordinate, Eyoub Sabri Bey, both a bloodthirsty and a corrupt man. His aim was always killing and, still more, plundering. During his time of office he accumulated great wealth.

This man, who had grown rich through the great amount of plunder that he had taken from the Armenians, never did any good to any Armenians. His religion and his conscience were money. The brutalities which he committed against the Armenians were not committed in the name of any patriotic ideal.

By the decrees of the Governor of Aleppo, Abdullhalik Bey, the representative of the General Deportations Committee, Abdullahad Nouri Bey had begun to make arrangements for the deportation; and when they had once begun working, crime succeeded crime. A new and awful order had arrived from the Ministry of the Interior, which gave them every license. And, as it was, they needed no license. These are the orders—

---

[4] Abdullahad Nouri Bey never took bribes. "Of course I like bribes," he would say, "but I am afraid to accept them. I am afraid that in the place of the money which enters into my pocket an Armenian —even if it is only one Armenian—will escape."

To the Government of Aleppo.

September[5] 9, 1915. — All rights of the Armenians to live and work on Turkish soil have been completely cancelled, and with regard to this the Government takes all responsibility on itself, and has commanded that even babes in the cradle are not to be spared. The results of carrying out this order have been seen in some provinces. In spite of this, for reasons unknown to us, exceptional measures are taken with 'Certain People,' and those people instead of being sent straight to the place of exile are left in Aleppo, whereby the Government is involved in an additional difficulty. Without listening to any of their reasoning, remove them thence—women or children, whatever they may be, even if they are incapable of moving; and do not let the people protect them, because, through their ignorance, they place material gains higher than patriotic feelings, and cannot appreciate the great policy of the Government in insisting upon this. Because instead of the indirect measures of extermination used in other places—such as severity, haste (in carrying out the deportations), difficulties of travelling and misery—direct measures can safely be used there, so work heartily.

General Orders have been communicated from the War Office to all the Commanders of the Army that they are not to interfere in the work of deportation.[6]

---

[5] In the 1920 text, "March."

[6] For a time the Commanding Officers of the military camps began to separate artisans from amongst the deportees, for the erection of military buildings. The deportation officials wrote to Constantinople complaining of this, and Talaat Pasha sends this order to say that the right to keep back artisans had been taken from the military officers.

Tell the officials that are to be appointed for that purpose that they must work to put into execution our real intent, without being afraid of responsibility. Please send cipher reports of the results of your activities every week.
Minister of the Interior,
TALAAT.

When this order came, the Deportations Committee of Aleppo had the right to do all sorts of things, under the direct orders of the Governor-General.

The reasons for leaving all the work of deportation in the hands of one man was that the orders given for putting barbarities into execution should be kept as secret as possible—so that many people might not know what was going on, and the crime might be committed in silence, without being noised abroad.

The camp where the deportees were gathered together was in the dreary height of Karlik, twenty minutes from Aleppo. From this place the deportees were sent to the desert. The lives of the Armenians who were there depended on the caprice of a police sergeant, or a deportation official.

Anyhow, there was no hope of life for any one who went a step beyond Aleppo. The whole line from Karlik to Der Zor was a track of misery—a graveyard. The officials in charge had been ordered not to abstain from any brutality which would cause death.

The two following telegrams prove this— both of them sent on behalf of Talaat Pasha, the Minister of the Interior.

We hear that some officials have been brought before a military tribunal (court martial) under the accusation of extortion and severity towards Certain People (the Armenians). Even though this may be a mere formality, it may lessen the energy of other officials. For this reason I command that you shall not allow such examinations.[7]

Minister of the Interior,
TALAAT.

To pay heed to the complaints lodged by 'Certain People' on all sorts of personal subjects will not only delay their dispatch to the desert but will also open the door to a series of actions which may entail political difficulties in the future. For this reason no notice should be taken of those applications, and orders must be given to this effect to the officials concerned.

Minister of the Interior,
TALAAT.

Instructions were subsequently received from the Minister of the Interior to the effect that letters or telegrams addressed to Governmental High Officials containing complaints should be received but not forwarded.

Thus the Armenian people who were in the deserts were condemned to certain death, and the executioners who were to carry out the work were just the men for it:—the Governor of Aleppo, Mustafa Abdullhalik, the representative of the General Deportations Committee, Abdullahad Nouri Bey, his

---

[7] Sergeant Rahmeddin, the Mudir of Abu-Harrar (one of the camps on the Euphrates; in the 1920 text, it reads 'Abu-Harrad'), who had become a terror to the Armenians, and often killed people with a great club which he invariably carried about with him, was summoned to Aleppo after many protests for a mock trial; but in accordance with this telegram he was sent back to his work again, without even being tried. On his return, as he was passing through Meskene to go to Abu-Harrar, he fired some revolver shots towards the deportees' camp, calling out, "You protested, and what was the result? Here I am again restored to my office." Naturally the brutalities practised by this man, whom the Armenians called "the bone-breaker," grew more numerous after his return.

11

colleague Eyoub Bey, the Deputy of the Ittihad, Jemal Bey, and a multitude of officials under them— one more bloodthirsty than another; all devoted heart and soul to the "sacred work," as the documents designated it.

THE MASSACRES of RES-UL-AIN

While the deportation of the deportees was carried on by railway, Kaimakam Yousouf Zia Bey reported that there was no more room for Armenians in Res-ul-Ain; that five or six hundred were dying every day, and that there was neither time to bury the dead nor to send the living further south.

He received an answer to the following effect.

> Hasten the deportations. In this way those who are not fit to leave will fall down and die at a few hours' distance from the town, and the town will get rid of both the living and the dead.

From the last reports of the local deportation officials and of the Kaimakam, it was understood that from 13,000 to 14,000 people died of starvation and sickness in four months.

The Armenians in Res-ul-Ain were in this condition, while in Aleppo the Turks were thinking out methods of exterminating them completely. Everything showed that Yousouf Zia Bey would not consent to become a tool for the carrying out of this crime. But there was a still greater obstacle—the Governor of Der Zor, Ali Souad Bey, who had done all he could in his official circle at Res-ul-Ain to mitigate the sufferings of the Armenians. He had directed them to pitch their tents at the foot of a hill near the village, and had, in a way, assigned a part of the village to those who still had a little money and could occupy themselves in commerce. In that quarter the Armenians had at once set up shops—tailors', shoemakers', grocers' and greengrocers' shops, and sixty bakeries. Amongst the deported Armenians there were a great many architects, builders, stone-masons, and other artisans. The military authorities were having a large hospital erected by them. Sixty master-builders were working at that hospital, and with their families received wages in return for their work.

Souad Bey had addressed the following words to the Kaimakam one day—

> Let us not ask why the Armenians are being deported; that is not our business. We can treat them as we like. If we like, we can protect and keep them, and profit by their industries. If we like, we can make an end of them. We cannot remove this misfortune which is weighing on them so heavily, but we can lighten it. I believe that by their labour these deserts will be turned into flowery fields, and in the place of these hovels, beautiful dwellings will be erected.

At the same time in Aleppo the plan to exterminate these people was being worked out.

The orders issued to the official commanding the deportations at Res-ul-Ain were not carried out. Abdullahad Nouri Bey himself went as far as Res-ul-Ain, and by worrying the official commanding the deportations, Arel Bey, he discovered that it was the Governor of Der Zor, Souad Bey himself, who had failed to carry out the order for driving the Armenians towards the desert.

On his return to Aleppo, Nouri Bey informed the Governor-General (Vali), Abdullhalik Bey of the truth, and he immediately sent the following order by cipher to Ali Souad Bey—

> It is contrary to the sacred purpose of the Government that thousands of Armenians should remain in Res-ul-Ain. Drive them into the desert.

Souad Bey answered—

There are no means of transport by which I can send the people away. If the purpose which you insist upon is slaughtering them, I can neither do it myself nor have it done.

Mustafa Abdullhalik Bey sent this telegram to Constantinople to the Ministry of the Interior, adding to it the following report concerning Souad Bey—

To the Ministry of the Interior.
Dec. 23, 1915.—We understand from the deputy of the general overseer of the Deportations Committee that the Armenians who have been sent to Res-ul-Ain are still there, and have built themselves good houses and established themselves comfortably; and that the person who is protecting them and allowing them to settle down is the Governor of Der Zor, All Souad Bey.

In spite of our having written again and again that the crowding of Armenians in a small but locally important town like Res-ul-Ain and the making of excuses such as the lack of means of transport, and so forth, for keeping them there lays a great responsibility upon us, yet we have seen no result.

The partiality which Ali Souad Bey has shown for them and the protection he has extended to them have reached amazing proportions. According to what we hear, he dresses and looks after some of the Armenian children himself, and he weeps and mourns with them over the sufferings of their parents. In this way the Armenians sent in that direction are enjoying a very happy existence, and they are indebted for this to Ali Souad Bey.

But as the continuation of this state of things will cause needless delays in the transport of deportees from Aleppo, we are addressing Your Excellency on the matter, begging that you will make all necessary arrangements.

MUSTAFA ABDULLHALIK,
Governor-General (Vali).

It was on the strength of this report that Ali Souad Bey was subsequently dismissed.

Affairs remained in this condition until February 1916. Then one of the most cruel and evil-reputed executors of the Armenian massacres arrived in Res-ul-Ain —a former Governor-General of Van, Jevdet Bey, brother-in-law of the Minister of War, Enver Pasha. After having accomplished the massacre in Van, he went to Moush, where he also supervised massacres; and thence he went to Bitlis, to complete the massacres of Mustafa Abdullhalik Bey. Having been appointed Governor of Adana, he was on his way there, and in February 1916 he reached Res-ul-Ain, where there were at that time about 50,000 Armenian deportees. The Kaimakam had gone out to meet him, with his suite.

Amongst the deportees there happened to be an Armenian doctor—Dr. Hreshdagian, who belonged to the staff of the Executive Committee of the Baghdad Railway. The doctor afterwards said that the first thing which attracted the attention of Jevdet Bey was the mound at whose base were the thousands of tents belonging to the Armenian camp.

Jevdet Bey thought that it was a military camp, and asked where those soldiers were going. The Kaimakam answered that those were not soldiers, but Armenian deportees. On hearing this, Jevdet Bey, not dreaming that there was an Armenian amongst his audience, exclaimed—

Are those dogs still in existence? I command you to slaughter them all!

The Kaimakam refused, saying that he could not shed the blood of so many innocent people, who had never done him any harm.

"Then you don't know what policy the Government is pursuing?"said Jevdet Bey, and he threatened to have him dismissed.

Suiting the action to the word, he summoned the chief of the telegraph office and immediately reported what had passed to Constantinople. The consequence could be nothing but a dismissal, and so it was. Yousouf Zia Bey was removed from Resul- Ain, and ten days later, at the beginning of March, a new Kaimakam arrived—a young man from Koch ana in Rumelia, Kerim Refi Bey. He was Jevdet Bey's man.

For the Armenian massacres the Government purposely appointed officials who, with their families, had suffered greatly during the deportations of the Balkan War, and had escaped to Constantinople. The bitterness of their past sufferings and the thirst for revenge was very strong in the hearts of these people. And that is the reason why they showed such fearful savagery, in spite of the fact that the Armenians had had no share in causing their sufferings. All through the Balkan wars the Armenian soldiers who were in the Turkish armies fought with great heroism on all the fronts, as all the Turkish commanders witnessed.

Not being able to wreak their vengeance on the Bulgarians, Serbians and Greeks, these Turkish officials wreaked it on the Armenians.

The new Kaimakam of Res-ul-Ain was one of these men, and he became an excellent tool in the hands of the jackals of Aleppo, before whom the ground was now quite clear, since they had succeeded in getting the dismissal of Ali Souad Bey, the Governor of Der Zor. On March 17, Kerim Bey began the deportations. This work had been entrusted to the Circassians, at the head of whom was the Mayor of Res-ul-Ain, Arslan Bey.

A guard was formed of the Circassians, ostensibly with the object of defending travellers from assault. This guard was armed. This company, however, which was supposed to be formed for protective purposes, had the office of slaughtering the deportees committed to their charge.

The order for the criminal deeds at Res-ul-Ain was given directly from Aleppo. This order was given to the chiefs of the guard. Some of them came to Aleppo and had interviews with Mustafa Abdullhalik Bey.[8] Four or five days after their return, the Kaimakam reported, by cipher-telegram, that they had arrived and received their orders. The massacres followed the deportations almost immediately, because they were committed in the neighbourhood, chiefly on the banks of the Jurjib and on the road to Shaddade. The Armenians were taken out in groups, and killed in the most brutal manner. Some of them used to escape occasionally, and come to Res-ul-Ain—it was not possible for them to go anywhere else—and they used to tell of the horrors. One can imagine how terrified the helpless people were who heard these stories, how they shuddered when they came with whips, revolvers and clubs to beat them and drive them out to the slaughter-houses. Neither the sick were spared, nor the children, nor the aged.

"Don't leave any of them alive—especially the children, down to five or seven years old; otherwise in a short time they will grow up, and seek to revenge themselves."[9]

Zeki Bey had arrived at Der Zor as governor, in the place of Ali Souad Bey; and, as the massacres had begun there, he

---

[8] Amongst these was the brother of Arslan Bey, Hussein Bey, who after the death of Arslan Bey (in the beginning of 1917) succeeded him as mayor in Res-ul-Ain. Both brothers played prominent parts in the massacres of Der Zor also. Hussein Bey used often to go to Aleppo to sell the property which he and his brother and others were constantly seizing from the deportees.

[9] This seemed to be a watchword. Every official in every place repeated it to the people who were to execute the massacres.

needed people to carry out his devilish work. To slaughter about 200,000 people is not an easy matter.

The colossal amount of labour needed had stupefied him. He had been obliged to call to his assistance all the Circassians who had executed the massacres of Res-ul-Ain. But still the butchers were not enough for the victims. Seeing that the Circassians would not be sufficient to complete the work, Zeki Bey had promised the Arab Ashirats of Der Zor the clothes of the victims, if they would come and help in the killing. And they had accepted the offer. Most of the Armenians were slaughtered by them.

The greater number of the officials both of the Executive Committee and of the constructional works were Armenians. The Government, on the pretext of being afraid that they would be unsuitable for the work, gave the following order—

> No. 801.
> To the Government of Aleppo.
> *Dec.* 26, 1915.—It has been decided that all Armenians working on the railway or on any other construction shall be sent to their places of deportation. The War 29 THE MEMOIRS OF NAIM BEY Office has given notice of this to the Commanders of deportation camps.
> Minister of the Interior,
> TALAAT.

Upon this their names were demanded from the military commissariats of the railway. Both the Railway Commissioner, Khairi Bey, and Jemal[10] Pasha showed great kindness with regard to this. Talaat Pasha's guilt is demonstrated by the fact that, although most of the officials on the railway were Armenians, and the Armenians had been treated so brutally during the four or five years of the war,

---

[10] In the 1920 text, "Jelal."

they had all worked faithfully the whole time. Nowhere on the line was there any accident through them.

But, a short time after, the question was raised again, and the following telegram arrived—

No. 840.
To the Government of Aleppo.
Jan. 16, 1916.—We hear that all along the line which runs between Intilli, Airan and Aleppo there are some forty or fifty thousand Armenians, mostly women and children. Those persons, who are causing a great deal of trouble by remaining on sites which are very important for the dispatch of troops, will be punished with the greatest severity. Therefore communicate with the Government of Adana, and send those Armenians to Aleppo immediately, without letting them go further. I am anxiously waiting to hear the result of this within a week.
Minister of the Interior,
TALAAT.

The following telegram, supplementing the foregoing one, was received the very same day.

To the Government of Aleppo.
Sequel to the telegram dated Jan. 16.
No. 840.
Do not deport the Armenian workers left at Intilli and Airan until the construction of the railway is completed. But, as it is not permissible for them to live with their families, billet them temporarily somewhere in the outskirts of Aleppo. The remaining women and children dispatch to the desert immediately, in compliance with the former telegram.
Minister of the Interior,
TALAAT.

When this order was executed the children of tender years were left behind under the trees, naked and hungry.

Herr Koppel[11] collected them and put them into cases prepared for dynamite, and took them to Intilli, where they were cared for in his orphanage. A few days later the German Director of the Baghdad Railway reproached him for this work of mercy.

The companies sent viâ Aintab and Marash were slaughtered all along the way until they reached Mardin, where none of them were to arrive. A number of them—500 people—were taken to Resul- Ain and there joined the 200 Armenian families that were left in the place and had not yet been massacred because the Circassians were occupied at Der Zor. But when the deportations at Der Zor were completed, and the massacres facilitated, the Circassians soon returned to Res-ul-Ain, and drove out the people left there, as well as those at Intilli, towards the neighbourhood of Shiddade. They were to be massacred with the last remnant of the Armenians of Der Zor.

While the massacres of Res-ul-Ain Intilli were being completed, the even more terrible slaughter, by means of which Zeki Bey was to exterminate the 200,000 Armenians deported to Der Zor, had begun. Zeki Bey was impatiently sending telegrams to the Government at Aleppo, asking that the Armenians in the neighbourhood of that town should be sent to him as soon as possible.

The real terror commenced when they began to drive the people who were in Aleppo and the neighbourhood towards Meskene. There was no end to the caravans. Bab, Maara and Moonbooj were completely emptied. Without regard to the severity of the weather, the Armenians were driven towards Meskene, often on foot, now and then on donkeys or camels.

---

[11] Herr Koppel was one of the Swiss engineers worthy of special mention, who did all in their power to save the lives of some of the Armenians working on the Baghdad railway line.

Even there also they might not stay. They must go to Der Zor—that was the decree.

The greater part of these deportees on the banks of the Euphrates were from the environs of Constantinople—from Rodosto, Nicomedia, Bardezag, Adabazar, Gezve and Konia—in a word, all the Armenians deported from along the line of the Anatolian Railway, and from Cesarea.

Everybody wondered why this new deportation was being made, and why the people were being driven towards Zor. But there was a still stronger reason for anxiety. News of the massacres at Resul- Ain had reached Meskene among other places. A massacre that went on for years could not remain secret even in the desert.

News had already arrived that no more deportees would be sent from the right bank of the Tigris—only from the left bank; and this in itself was a death-sentence for the caravans about to depart; for from that bank as far as Rakka they would have to travel through waterless deserts, where they would certainly die of the heat or of hunger and thirst. The El-Jezireh, as the left bank of the river was called, was the road to the tomb.

The deportees coming from Bab increased the terror by bringing with them the following telegraphic order, which the Governor-General of Aleppo and the Mayor sent to the Kaimakam of Bab—

Very urgent and secret. "Do not keep back even condemned Armenians or those accused or arrested by the police; send them down to Der Zor at once.

The Turkish soldiers often pointed out to the Armenians, with devilish sarcasm, troops of Indians, and especially English prisoners that were being deported to Nisibin, to work on the construction of the railway. Their condition was no better than that of the Armenians. They had been starving for days, and most of them were worn out and incapable of walking. They were dragging themselves along the road, and many of them would fall down then and there, often under revolver shots. They had neither shoes nor clothing. Pale, emaciated and bent, they were more like shadows than men. And the Turks pointed out those caravans to the Armenians, and said: "Here are the people you worship—here are those with whom you sympathise and for whom you were sacrificed. Call them—call them to liberate you!"

Old women took out bags of earth which they had brought with them from their distant homes—the earth which had been sanctified by all the martyrdom and bloodshed through which they had brought and kept it. Feeling that they were going to die, they distributed that earth amongst those who had none. They placed it in their bosoms, so that when they died in this strange land, they might at least close their eyes in the illusion that they were dying in the embrace of their native soil.

All the orders of the Government said— "Join them on to the caravans and send them." The meaning of this ambiguous saying was: "Send them to the desert." But even in the desert there was no fixed place for the Armenian deportees. They always had to get up, walk, and move on, no one knew whither. It was enough that they should not stay long in one place, and should wear themselves out by walking.

Before even the idea of the Yildirim army had been conceived, the Government sent the following telegram to Aleppo—

> No. 723.
> A cipher-telegram from the Ministry of the Interior, sent to the Government of Aleppo.
> *Dec.* 8, 1915.—Send the Armenians— those in the neighbourhood of Aleppo first—without delay, to their place of deportation, and report concerning this.
> Minister of the Interior,
> TALAAT.

At the beginning of the deportations, at least, the villages around Aleppo were appointed to be dwelling-places for the Armenians. Great numbers of Armenians were settled in those villages. On receipt of this telegram, mounted gendarmes were sent round the environs of Aleppo, who began to turn the people out of the villages by means of many cruelties, driving them towards Meskene, where most of them were put to death.

It is worth while to recall in this connection that the order for the general deportation of the Armenians came after Marshal Mackenson had pierced the Russian front, when the crushing of Russia, and consequently ultimate victory, seemed assured to the Turks.

Instructions were given from Aleppo to try and keep the deportees hungry and thirsty on the way, so as to diminish their numbers as much as possible. On January 20, 1916, Abdullahad Nouri Bey wrote to the chief official of the Deportations Committee of Bab, Mouharrem Bey—

No. 344.

Jan. 20, 1916. — Doubtless you appreciate the confidence which the Government has in you, and you realise the importance of the work entrusted to you. You are not to permit one single Armenian to remain in Bab. Your severity and promptitude with regard to the deportations can alone assure the success of the scheme which we are pursuing. Only you must take care that no corpses are left by the roadsides. Let us know by post the maximum remuneration which you propose to pay to the men whom you appoint for this work.

Do not trouble about means of transport. The deportees can go on foot.

The weekly death-rate sent to us during these last few days was not satisfactory. It is evident from this that those people (the Armenians) are living quite comfortably there.

The dispatch of the deportees must not be like a journey. Do not listen to protests or lamentations. The Government has sent the necessary instructions to the Kaimakam as well.

ABDULLAHAD NOURI.

Abdullahad Nouri Bey subsequently issued the following order—

"No official will be held responsible for any severities connected with the deportations of Armenians."

In accordance with the foregoing instructions, all the deportees in Bab were to be driven out within twenty-four hours.

The number of deaths was reported to Constantinople by cipher-telegrams once a fortnight.

The Government demanded that the life and honour of the Armenians should be destroyed. They no longer had any right to exist. Talaat Pasha wrote—

It is necessary to punish those who wish to ensure the existence of the Armenians, who have for centuries been an element of danger to Turkey, and have recently tried to inundate the whole of our country with blood. Send secret instructions to the Officials.

At one moment, when the joy of the Turks was at its height, the deportations were so harsh in Aleppo that the gendarmes and police would go into the houses and tie up like pigs and drive out the poor Armenians, who had no refuge but God, and were hiding themselves through the fear of death.

One day a poor man presented a petition to say that, while his whole family had been suffering from typhus, they had thrown them all out into the street, put them into dust-carts and sent them out of town to Karlok. The wretched man begged and implored with sobs and tears that they would at least give him ten days' grace, He did not know that he was condemned to death; no one would pity him. During my term of office 10,000 petitions were given in to our office from the Armenian deportees. I did not see any notice taken of even ten of them.

A woman from Diarbekir was seen carrying a plate with the Armenian coat-of-arms on it. She was brought before the General Deportations Committee, and asked where she had got that plate.[12] The woman answered that it had been in her house a long time, and she did not know whence it was brought. She was taken to a cell in the gendarmerie, where she was tortured eight or ten days, in order to find out where she had got the plate. But the poor woman did not know. She died in the midst of those tortures, which were aggravated by hunger.

Thus, after having witnessed hundreds of thousands of such dramas in Aleppo, I was sent to Meskene as an official of the Deportations Committee. When I was about to depart, Eyoub Bey called me and said:

> We have not been satisfied with any of the officials sent to Meskene. You Kare been in the work, and you are familiar with the orders that have been sent. See that you do not let those people (the Armenians) live. When necessary, kill them with your own hand. Killing them is an amusement.

---

[12] All kinds of objects and pictures bearing this coat-of-arms were sold freely all over Turkey after the Constitution was established. During the deportations all those who possessed any of these objects were punished with death.

I went to Meskene; I heard of the crimes committed. I remained there two months and only once deported a company. Their number could not have exceeded thirty. While I was still at Aleppo, the following cipher-telegram had arrived from Constantinople—

A cipher-telegram from the Ministry of the Interior, sent to the Government of Aleppo.

Dec. 1, 1915.—In spite of the that it is necessary above all to work for the extermination of the Armenian Clergy, we hear that they are being sent to suspicious places like Syria and Jerusalem. Such a permit is an unpardonable delinquency. The place of exile of such seditious people is annihilation. I recommend you to act accordingly.

Minister of the Interior,

TALAAT.

When I went to Meskene the old Bishop of Nicomedia (Izmit) was there. He sat in a small tent, and spent the time in thinking of his fate. No one knows how the attention of the Director of the Deportations Committee was called to this man, who was incapable of doing any harm to any one.

I received a note to the effect that the Bishop of Izmit was there; why had they kept him? he must be deported, so that he might fall down at some corner of the road and die. I could not say that it would not do, or refuse to send him. But we did not send him.

Another time two priests had been sent to Meskene. The order given concerning these two was very severe. It openly commanded that they should be killed. I did not deport those two priests, however, I kept them where they were. I do not remember their names, but I think that both of them are in Aleppo now.

Meskene was filled with skeletons, from one end to the other. It looked like a real valley of dry bones.

Two hundred thousand Armenians were sent out on the road from Aleppo to Meskene and Res-ul-Ain alone, and only about five or six thousand of this great multitude survived. The babies were thrown into the Euphrates and drowned. The women were killed with bayonets or revolvers at different points of the road by the savagery of the gendarmes or the people.

THE MASSACRES OF DER ZOR

A discharged postmaster of Der Zor described the beginning of the massacres at Zor as follows. A cipher-telegram arrived at Der Zor from the Ministry of the Interior, saying,

> An end has been made of the deportations; begin to work according to the previous order, and let it be done as rapidly as possible.

The massacre began two days after the cipher-telegram arrived. At the end of July, Zeki Bey sent the following telegram to Aleppo—

> Cipher-telegram from the Government of Zor sent to the Governor-General of Aleppo.
> *July* 31,1916.—In accordance with the order sent to me from the Committee, when the deportations of the Armenian deportees from Aleppo have been somewhat slackened, the dwelling-place of the Armenians[13] that are here will be changed. Please let

---

[13] The meaning of the sentence in this telegram— "the dwelling-place of the Armenians that are here will be changed"—is that they will be massacred, and as a matter of fact the massacres which Zeki Bey was so anxious to consummate had already begun with the removal of the Armenians all along the banks of the Euphrates to the slaughter-house of Der Zor.

me know how long the deportation of the deportees
is to continue.
Governor,
ZEKI.

The people were driven out of Der Zor in batches, under
the pretext of being sent to Mousul. But they were unable to
go beyond Sheddade. Zeki Bey selected principally the
deserts of Marat and Souvar on the road to Sheddade, and as
it was impossible to wipe out so many people by slaughtering
them, he created an artificial famine, during which the people
first ate the donkeys, dogs and cats, then the carcases of
horses and dogs, and finally, when there was nothing else left
to eat, they began to devour human corpses, more especially
corpses of small children.

In the desert some ownerless and hungry children saw a
cauldron on a fire at a camp and thought that it was meat
cooking; they took off the lid of the cauldron and stole a
piece. It was a little child's hand they had stolen.

A girl was ill in bed, from having had nothing to eat for
several days. Her mother was watching beside her. The smell
of cooking meat came from somewhere near. Doubtless they
were cooking the corpse of some child.

"Mother, go and ask for a piece, I can stand it no longer,"
said the girl. The mother went, but shortly returned empty-
handed.

"Wouldn't they give any?" said the girl. "Mother, if I die,
don't give them any of my flesh. Eat it yourself."

In this way the children were accustomed, while still alive,
to the idea that their corpses would be eaten after their death.

A chemist who had some poison with him made pills of it,
and fortunate people used to buy them, so as to be liberated a
moment earlier from those unspeakable tortures.

In order to keep the enthusiasm of the Turks for massacre
up to the mark, Zeki Bey would often bend down from his
horse, take hold of a small child by its arm, turn it round once

or twice in the air and dash it to the ground, killing and breaking it to pieces; and he would say to his followers:

> Don't think that I have killed an innocent being. Even the new-born babes of this people (Armenians) are criminals, for they will carry the seeds of vengeance in themselves. If you wish to ensure to-morrow, kill even their children.

And they spared none.

Only a few of the good-looking girls were saved from the massacres. After a week or two, those girls were sent on camels to Res-ul-Ain, towards Mardin, where they were often sold for five piastres (one shilling). In this way was completed the massacre of Der Zor, in which nearly all the Armenians who had been deported into the desert were wiped out—more than 200,000 people.

A month before the declaration of war by Turkey the Turkish War Office entered into negotiations with a delegation of eight Georgians who met the Turkish officials at Trebizond.

The Constantinople newspapers of April 15 report the proceedings in the Turkish Parliament with regard to these negotiations as follows—

> *The President.* Of whom did that delegation consist?
>
> *Yousouf Riza Bey.* The chief of the delegation was Tseretelli, and Colonel Terel was with him. It was promised to these two and to their three companions that an independent Georgian state should be founded, in which all the eight should have positions as ministers.
>
> *The President.* Who made that promise?
>
> *Yousouf Riza Bey.* Turkey, in her own name and in that of the German Empire.

The President. What were the conditions to be?

Yousouf Riza Bey. The Georgians in the Caucasus were to revolt, being provided with arms and munitions by us, and were to cut off the Russian line of retreat; they were also to destroy the railway lines and to blow up the arsenals and munition factories.

The President. Had Turkey declared war then?

Yousouf Riza Bey. No!

The President. Where were you when war was declared?

Yousouf Riza Bey. In a Russian town.

The President. That means that your centre (the centre of the Ittihad) had already decided to enter the war, since you were already over the Russian frontier before war was declared."

The Armenian Patriarch at Constantinople had, on April 11, 1915, made representations on behalf of the Armenians exiled from Constantinople to the Grand Vizier, Said Halim Pasha, whose reply— verbatim—was as follows—

Before the war you approached the Entente Powers, wishing to sever yourselves from the Ottoman Empire. What is happening to the Armenians is the result of a scheme which will be carried out.

Some of the following dispatches emanating from the Ittihad Committee bear as signatures merely an initial.

February[14] 25, 1915.—To the delegate at Adana, Jemal Bey.

The only force in Turkey that is able to frustrate the political life of the Ittihad and Terakke[15] is the

---

[14] In the original 1920 text, "March."

Armenians. From news which has frequently been received lately from Cairo, we learn that the Dashnagtzoutiun[16] is preparing a decisive attack against the Jemiet.

If we examine minutely the historical circumstances of the past we shall find that all the storms which have obstructed the patriotic efforts of the Jemiet are the result of the seeds of discord sown by the Armenians.

It will be forbidden to help or protect any Armenian.

The Jemiet has decided to save the fatherland from the ambition of this cursed race, and to take on its own patriotic shoulders the stain which will blacken Ottoman history.

The Jemiet, unable to forget all old scores and past bitterness, full of hope for the future, has decided to annihilate all Armenians living in Turkey, without leaving a single one alive, and it has given the Government a wide scope with regard to this.

---

[15] The Committee of Union and Progress, which is also called "Jemiet"(or "Assembly"). It is necessary to explain that in those days there were two Governments in Turkey—one was the official one, the Cabinet of Said Halim Pasha, and the other that of the Ittihad Committee, which, although unofficial, was a more real and influential power, for it held the official Government under the strictest control. It had special delegates in all the provinces—they were generally called "Responsible Secretaries," and these delegates superintended all activities, especially the Armenian deportations and massacres.

[16] The "attack" of the Dashnagtzoutiun mentioned in the first paragraph of this letter was nothing new, and had no connection with the European war.

What the letter calls an "attack" was the union which the Dashnagtzoutiun and other Armenian political parties formed in Egypt to press for reforms in Turkey, at the time of the Balkan War, when the Powers were already stirring up the question.

Of course the Government will give the necessary injunctions about the necessary massacres to the Governors. All the delegates of the Ittihad and Terakke will do their utmost to push on this matter.

The property left will be temporarily confiscated by any means that the Govern ment thinks fit, with the intention of its being sold afterwards and the money used for reorganising the Jemiet on a broader basis, and for patriotic purposes.

With regard to this, if you deem it necessary, demand an explanation from the Executive Committees which are to be formed. If you see anything in the administration which is not in order, you can apply either to the Governors-General or to us.

The second dispatch shows that, when the Turkish Government finished with the Armenians, they were going to undertake the extermination of other races—Greeks, Syrians and Arabs.

To Jemal Bey, delegate at Adana.

March[17] 18, 1915.—It is the duty of all of us to effect on the broadest lines the realisation of the noble project of wiping out of existence the Armenians who have for centuries been constituting a barrier to the Empire's progress in civilisation. For this reason we must take upon ourselves the whole responsibility, saying 'come what may,' and appreciating how great is the sacrifice which has enabled the Government to enter the world war, we must work so that the means adopted may lead to the desired end.

---

[17] In the original 1920 text, "November."

As announced in our dispatch dated February 18,[18] the Jemiet has decided to uproot and annihilate the various forces which have for centuries been an obstacle in its way, and to this end it is obliged to resort to Very bloody methods. Be assured that we ourselves were horrified at the contemplation of these methods, but the Jemiet sees no other way of ensuring the stability of its work.

We are criticised and called upon to be merciful; such simplicity is nothing short of stupidity. For those who will not co-operate with us we will find a place that will wring their delicate heart-strings.

I again recall to your memory the question of the property left. It is very important. Do not let its distribution escape your vigilance; always examine the accounts and the use made of the proceeds.

(See the original, Plate I.)

A cipher-telegram from the Ministry of the Interior, addressed to the Government of Aleppo.

From interventions which have recently been made by the American Ambassador of Constantinople on behalf of his Government, it appears that the American consuls are obtaining information by secret means. In spite of our assurances that the (Armenian) deportations will be accomplished in safety and comfort, they remain unconvinced. Be careful that events attracting attention shall not take place in connection with those (Armenians) who are near the cities, and other centres. From the point of view of the present policy it is most important that foreigners who are in those parts shall be persuaded that the expulsion of the

---

[18] In the original 1920 text, "8."

33

Armenians is in truth only deportation. For this reason it is important that, to save appearances, a show of gentle dealing shall be made for a time, and the usual measures be taken in suitable places. It is recommended as very important that the people who have given such information shall be arrested and handed over to the military authorities for trial by court-martial.

Minister of the Interior,
TALAAT.

Nov. 21, 1915. — P.S. — Without mentioning the cipher-telegram see the Director. Are there really such meddlesome people? In accordance with the order of the committee, let the operations conducted there be a little moderate. To the representative of the General Committee,

Governor-General,
MUSTAFA ABDULLHALIK.
(See the original, Plate II.)

I was certain of the existence of such people, and had repeatedly requested the Chief of Police to make the necessary investigations, but it was no good. If strict injunctions are sent to him direct from the Government, it may have some effect. We give you full authority with regard to this.

Representative of the General Committee,
ABDULLAHAD NOURI.

A cipher-telegram from the Ministry of the Interior, sent to the Government of Aleppo (No. 745)—

> *Dec.* 11, 1915.—We hear that the correspondents of Armenian newspapers travelling in those parts have faked some letters and photographs showing certain criminal actions, which they have given to the American consuls. Arrest and destroy such dangerous persons.
> Minister of the Interior,
> TALAAT.

The following cipher-telegram further demonstrates the anxiety of the Government—

> No. 809.
> To the Government of Aleppo.
> *Dec.* 29, 1915.—We hear that there are numbers of alien officers on the roads who have seen the corpses of the abovementioned people (the Armenians) and are photographing them. It is recommended as very important that those corpses should at once be buried, and not left so exposed.
> Minister of the Interior,
> TALAAT.

> No. 502.
> To the Government of Aleppo.
> *Sept.* 3, 1915.—We recommend that the operations which we have ordered you to make shall be first carried out on the men of the said people (the Armenians), and that you shall subject the women and children to them also. Appoint reliable officials for this.
> Minister of the Interior,
> TALAAT.

No. 537.

To the Government of Aleppo.

Sept. 29, 1915.—We hear that some of the people and officials are marrying Armenian women. We strictly prohibit this, and urgently recommend that these women shall be picked out and sent away (to the desert).

Minister of the Interior,
TALAAT.

No. 691.

To the Government of Aleppo.

Nov. 23, 1915.—Destroy by secret means the Armenians of the Eastern Provinces who pass into your hands there.

Minister of the Interior,
TALAAT.

No. 820.

To the Government of Aleppo.

Jan. 4, 1916.—It is decreed that all Armenians coming from the north shall be sent straight to their place of deportation, without passing through any town or village on the way.

Minister of the Interior,
TALAAT.

A cipher-telegram sent from the Government of Aleppo to the Government of Aintab—

Jan. 11,1916.—We hear that there are Armenians from Sivas and Kharput in your vicinity. Do not give them any opportunity of settling there, and, by the methods you are acquainted with, which have already been communicated to you, do what is necessary and report the result.

Governor-General,
MUSTAFA ABDULLHALIK.

From the Government of Aintab.
To the Government of Aleppo.
An answer to the cipher-telegram of Jan. 11, 1916.

Jan. 18, 1916.—It has been ascertained that there are about five hundred people from the said provinces in the vicinity of Roum Kale, which is under our jurisdiction. The Kaimakam of Roum Kale reports that most of them are women and children, and that, in accordance with the methods with which the Turkish officials were acquainted, communicated to them earlier, these women and children have been sent under Kurdish guards, with the understanding that they are never to return.

GOVERNOR AHMET.

To the Government of Aleppo.
Feb. 20, 1916. — The military authorities proclaim the necessity of using those of the aforesaid people (the Armenians) that are of military age, for military service. We think that it will not be possible to send them to the war-zones, and, as it is not permissible for them to remain in the town either, we permit you to use them outside the town for road-making, or any other necessary work, on condition that their families shall be sent away with the rest of the deportees. Special orders have been sent from the War Office to the Military Authorities

to this effect. Consequently, communicate with them, and work in harmony with them.

Minister of the Interior,

TALAAT.

No. 57.

To the General Committee for settling the deportees.

Jan. 10, 1916.—Enquiries having been made, it is understood that hardly ten per cent of the Armenians subjected to the general deportations have reached the places destined for them; the rest have died from natural causes, such as hunger and sickness. We inform you that we are working to bring about the same result with regard to those who are still alive, by using severe measures.

ABDULLAHAD NOURI.

To the General Committee for settling the deportees.

Feb. 26, 1916.—I report for your information that hardly a quarter of the Armenians sent to the desert have arrived at their destination, with the exception of those sent to Syria as artisans.[19] The rest have died from natural causes on the way. We have taken in hand measures to send also those that were for various reasons left in Aleppo.

ABDULLAHAD NOURI.

---

[19] It was a common saying in Constantinople, "When you build a house and need workmen, you will see that not a single Turk will present himself. But if you are going to pull down a house, all who present themselves will be Turks." It was the Armenians who built all the barracks, hospitals, inns, etc., on the Meskene-Der Zor line.

No. 76.

To the Committee for settling the deportees.

In answer to the telegram dated March 3, 1916.

March 7, 1916. — We understand from information received that 35,000 Armenians have died in the vicinity of Bab and Meskene from various causes, 10,000 in Karluk (the place of deportation from Aleppo), 20,000 at Dipsi, Abu Harrar, and Hamam, and 35,000 in Res-ul-Ain— 100,000 in all.

ABDULLAHAD NOURI.

No. 51.

To the General Committee for settling the deportees.

Dec. 13, 1915.—It was ordered by telegrams dated September 9 and November 20, 1915, sent by the Ministry of the Interior, that certain persons therein named should be arrested. Having ascertained that they are at Res-ul-Ain, we inform you that the necessary operations have been carried out, in accordance with the order received from the Ministry, delivered to us by an official specially sent from here.

ABDULLAHAD NOURI.

No. 603.

To the Government of Aleppo.

Nov. 5, 1915.—We are informed that the little ones belonging to the Armenians from Sivas, Mamuret-ul-Aziz, Diarbekir and Erzeroum are adopted by certain Moslem families and received as servants when they are left alone through the death of their parents. We inform you that you are to collect all such children in your province and send them to the places of deportation, and also to give the necessary orders regarding this to the people.

Minister of the Interior,

TALAAT.

P.S.—See the Chief of the Police about it.

The Representatives of the General Deportations Committee, Governor-General,

MUSTAFA ABDULLHALIK.

To the Government of Aleppo.

Sept. 21, 1915.—There is no need for an orphanage. It is not the time to give way to sentiment and feed the orphans, prolonging their lives. Send them away to the desert and inform us.

Minister of the Interior,

TALAAT.

No. 31.

To the General Committee for settling the deportees.

Nov. 26,1915.—There were more than four hundred children in the orphanage. They will be added to the caravans and sent to their places of exile.

ABDULLAHAD NOURI.

To the Government of Aleppo.

Jan. 15, 1916.—We hear that certain orphanages which have been opened receive also the children of the Armenians. Whether this is done through ignorance of our real purpose, or through contempt of it, the Government will regard the feeding of such children or any attempt to prolong their lives as an act entirely opposed to its purpose, since it considers the survival of these children as detrimental. I recommend that such children shall not be received into the orphanages, and no attempts are to be made to establish special orphanages for them.

Minister of the Interior,
TALAAT.

(See the original, Plate III.)

No. 830.

A cipher-telegram from the Ministry of the Interior addressed to the Government of Aleppo.

Collect and keep only those orphans who cannot remember the tortures to which their parents have been subjected. Send the rest away with the caravans.

Minister of the Interior,
TALAAT.

No. 853. "A cipher-telegram from the Ministry of the Interior addressed to the Government of Aleppo

Jan. 23, 1916.—At a time when there are thousands of Moslem refugees and the widows of our martyrs[20] are in need of food and protection, it is not expedient to incur extra expenses by feeding the children left by Armenians, who will serve no purpose except that of giving trouble in the future. It is necessary that these children should be turned out of your vilayet and sent with the caravans to the places of deportation. Those that have been kept till

---

[20] The Turks call their soldiers fallen in the war Shekid, or martyrs.

now are also to be sent away, in compliance with our previous orders, to Sivas.

Minister of the Interior,

TALAAT.

(See the original, Plate IV.)

No. 63.

To the General Committee for settling the deportees.

By continuing the deportation of the orphans to their destinations during the intense cold, we are ensuring their eternal rest. Consequently we beg you to send us the sum which we asked for.

To the Government of Aleppo.

Collect the children of the Armenians who, by order of the War Office, have been gathered together and cared for by the military authorities. Take them away on the pretext that they are to be looked after by the Deportations Committee, so as not to arouse suspicion. Destroy them and report."

Minister of the Interior,

TALAAT.

No. 544.

Cipher-telegram from the Ministry of the Interior to the Government of Aleppo.

Oct. 3, 1915.—The reason why the sanjak of Zor was chosen as a place of deportation is explained in a secret order dated September 2,1915, No. 1843. As all the crimes to be committed by the population along the way against the Armenians will serve to effect the ultimate purpose of the Government, there is no need for legal proceedings with regard to these.

The necessary instructions have also been sent to the Governments of Zor and Ourfa.

Minister of the Interior,

TALAAT.

No. 745.

Cipher-telegram from the Ministry of the Interior addressed to the Government of Aleppo.

Dec. 9, 1915.—There is nothing wrong in accepting the telegrams sent to Government offices by the Armenians, complaining and protesting against the deeds done to them. But it would be a waste of time to examine them. Tell those who protest to claim their lost rights when they reach their place of exile.

Minister of the Interior,

TALAAT.

To the Government of Aleppo.

Sept. 16, 1915.—It was at first communicated to you that the Government, by order of the Jemiet (the Ittihad Committee) had decided to destroy completely all the Armenians living in Turkey. Those who oppose this order and decision cannot remain on the official staff of the Empire. An end must be put to their existence, however criminal the measures taken may be, and no regard must be paid to either age or sex nor to conscientious scruples.

Minister of the Interior,

TALAAT.

No. 762.

To the Government of Aleppo.

Answer to the telegram of Dec. 2,1915.

Dec. 17, 1915.—Communicate to those who wish to save themselves from the general deportations by becoming Moslems that they must become Moslems in their places of exile.

Minister of the Interior,
TALAAT.

To the Government of Aleppo.

Feb. 8, 1916.—After having fulfilled its duties in examining and acquiring papers concerning the seditious ideas and doings of the, Armenians[21] the Committee sent to Ourfa under Mustafa Nail Effendi will make investigations in the towns of Aintab and Kilis also, which are in your provinces. Consequently send secret instructions to the right quarters so that the necessary steps may be taken to facilitate their efforts and ensure their success.

Minister of the Interior,
TALAAT.

---

[21] The Committee referred to in this telegram spread its activities everywhere, and finally published a large volume in which it tried to prove by the most ridiculous lies that the Armenians had really threatened the existence of the Ottoman Empire, and that the Government had been obliged in consequence to deport them. The strongest evidence in this book consists of the photographs of arms collected from the Armenians. Amongst them were some photographs of bombs found in the provinces near Constantinople. These bombs were prepared by the Armenian party known as the "Dashnagtzagans" in co-operation with the Ittihad Committee, so that, in case a reaction took place in Turkey, as had been the case shortly after the Constitution was proclaimed on March 81, 1909, the Armenians and the Young Turks might be able to fight side by side against the Reactionaries.

It was in Germany that certain albums were first published by the Turkish Government, with the object of proving the guilt of the Armenians.

No. 563.

A cipher-telegram from the Ministry of the Interior to the Government of Aleppo.

Oct. 12, 1915.—Prepare to send within a week the papers demanded by cipher order.

Minister of the Interior,

TALAAT.

A cipher-telegram from the War Office sent to all the commanding officers of the army.

Feb. 27, 1918. — In view of present circumstances, the Imperial Government has issued an order for the extermination of the whole Armenian race. The following operations are to be made with regard to them:—

(1) All the Armenians in the country who are Ottoman subjects, from five years of age upwards, are to be taken out of the towns and slaughtered.

(2) All the Armenians serving in the Imperial Armies are to be separated from their divisions without making any disturbance; they are to be taken into solitary places away from the public eye, and shot.

(3) Armenian officers in the army are to be imprisoned in the barracks belonging to their regiments until further orders.

Forty-eight hours after these three orders are communicated to the commanders of each regiment, a special order will be issued for their execution. You are not to undertake any operations except those indispensable for the execution of these orders.

Representative of the High Command, and Minister of War,

ENVER.

The official telegrams which we have published have already thrown much light upon this matter. The orders which constantly came from Constantinople with regard to letting crimes committed on the road against the Armenian deportees go unpunished, and encouraging them, are certainly not calculated to establish the innocence of the people.

Even Turkish elements like those who, in the time of Hamid II, had refused to take part in the massacres and had in some places protected their Armenian neighbours, enthusiastically welcomed the Government's project of exterminating the Armenians. The Ittihad had spread its poison even as far as those strata—it had succeeded in awakening in all the Turks and Kurds the instinct of massacre and plunder.

"The war had scarcely commenced," writes Naim Bey in his memoirs, "when hunger and misery began to show themselves in an already incapacitated Turkey. It was necessary to feed and deceive the people, and that could be done by means of the money and property that the Armenians would leave behind. In the provinces of Erzeroum, Bitlis, Diarbekir, Mamurat-ul-Aziz, and Sivas, the massacre and plundering of the Armenians had already begun. This occupation made the people forget everything else. It was necessary to divert Syria and Mesopotamia also. The roads and plains of Mesopotamia and the desert of Syria were filled with Armenians. Much of the enormous wealth which the Armenians had earned through centuries of honourable work was seized. What was left of it was to be lost in those deserts, the inhabitants of which soon understood that the Armenians were being sent to them as victims. At the beginning they made feeble assaults, but, when they realised what the State policy was, they proceeded to wholesale slaughter and plunder.

The Ittihad Committee, the people and all the Moslem population in Turkey had a hand in this crime.

Kemal Bey was the Governor of Yozghat at the time of the deportations, and he organised one of the most terrible of the massacres in that region. After the troops of the Entente had entered Constantinople, the military tribunal condemned him to death, and he was hanged. The Turkish people organised great demonstrations to protest against this punishment, and was not ashamed to designate as a "martyr "this man who was nothing better than a murderer, having brought about the death of some 60,000 people.

The Turkish people behaved in the same way at the time that the members of the Ittihad Committee were being tried. This trial was rather a political ruse than a work of justice. The present Government in Turkey simply wanted to throw dust in the eyes of Europe. But the pressure of the Turkish people soon forced them to put an end to this sham, and the trial stopped without any result.

Let us hear what a Turk has to say about this. At the beginning of the present year, when the trial of a few of the secondary criminals was commenced in Constantinople, a Turkish newspaper, the Sdbah, published an article over the signature of the editor, Ali Kemal Bey, which treated this trial with well-grounded scepticism. And what he said with regard to this was a condemnation not only of the Ittihad Committee, not only of the Turkish Government, but of the whole Turkish people.

"We think," writes Ali Kemal Bey,[22]

> that those who know how to judge conscientiously and without bias will give a verdict in our favour. What are the facts of the case'? Four or five years ago a crime universal and unique in history was being perpetrated in our country. Taking into consideration the gigantic magnitude and extent

---

[22] Ali Kemal Bey was, at the time he wrote this, the Turkish Minister of the Interior.

47

of the crime, it could not have been committed by four or five people, but proportionately by hundreds of thousands. If the victims had been 300,000 instead of 600,000—if they had been even 200,000 or 100,000, a hundred, five hundred, or even a thousand criminals could not have wiped out so many people. It is already a proved fact that this crime was mapped out and decreed by the General Centre of the Ittihad. After the programme of the crime had been drawn up by certain bodies, it was carried out by Governors- General and Governments—that is, by Government officials, by the police and by the people. Now, is it not a contempt of justice to let loose on the one hand a multitude of great and small criminals, and on the other to arrest only the Governors-General of Diarbekir, Sivas and Kharput (who were in any case not tried), and a few subordinate officials?—*Sabah*, January 28, 1919.

APPENDIX

AN OPEN LETTER TO PRESIDENT WILSON

BY

ARMIN T. WEGNER

(A German eye-witness of the Armenian massacres)
Berlin,
January 1919.

MR. PRESIDENT, In your message to Congress of January 8, 1918, you made a demand for the liberation of all non-Turkish peoples in the Ottoman Empire. One of these peoples is the Armenian nation. It is on behalf of the Armenian nation that I am addressing you.

As one of the few Europeans who have been eye-witnesses of the dreadful destruction of the Armenian people from its beginning in the fruitful fields of Anatolia up to the wiping out of the mournful remnants of the race on the banks of the Euphrates, I venture to claim the right of setting before you these pictures of misery and terror which passed before my eyes during nearly two years, and which will never be obliterated from my mind. I appeal to you at the moment when the Governments allied to you are carrying on peace negotiations in Paris, which will determine the fate of the world for many decades. But the Armenian people is only a small one among several others; and the future of greater States more prominent in the world's eye is hanging in the balance. And so there is reason to fear that the significance of a small and extremely enfeebled nation may be obscured by the influential and selfish aims of the great European states, and that with regard to Armenia there will be a repetition of the old game of neglect and oblivion of which she has so often been the victim in the course of her history.

But this would be most lamentable, for no people in the world has suffered such wrongs as the Armenian nation. The

Armenian Question is a question for Christendom, for the whole human race.

The Armenian people were victims of this War. When the Turkish Government, in the Spring of 1915, set about the execution of its monstrous project of exterminating a million of Armenians, all the nations of Europe were unhappily bleeding to exhaustion, owing to the tragic blindness of their mutual misunderstanding, and there was no one to hinder the lurid tyrants of Turkey from carrying on to the bitter end those revolting atrocities which can only be likened to the acts of a criminal lunatic. And so they drove the whole people— men, women, hoary elders, children, expectant mothers and dumb sucklings—into the Arabian desert, with no other object than to let them starve to death.

For a long time, Europeans had been wont to regard Siberia as one of the most inhospitable regions in the world; to be condemned to live there was regarded as a most severe punishment. And yet, even in that place, there are fertile lands and, despite the cold of its winters, the climate is healthy. But what is Siberia compared with the Mesopotamian Steppes? There we find a long tract of land without grass, without trees, without cattle, covered with stunted weeds, a country where the only inhabitants are Arab Bedouins, destitute of all pity; a stretch of grey limestone plains several miles in extent, bare wastes of rock and stone, ruined river banks, exposed to the rays of a merciless sun, ceaseless autumn rains, and frosty winter nights, leaving sheets of ice behind them. Except its two large rivers there is no water. The few small villages scarcely suffice to feed a handful of Bedouins, who, in their wretched poverty, regard any traveller as a welcome prey. From the dwellings which their race had held for more than two thousand years, from all parts of the Empire, from the stony passes of the mountain region to the shores of the Sea of Marmora and the palmy oases of the South, the Armenians were driven into this desolate waste, with the alleged purpose of forcibly transplanting them from their homes to a strange land—a purpose which, even had it been the real one, is repugnant to every human feeling. The men were struck down in batches, bound together with chains and ropes, and thrown into the river or rolled down the mountain with fettered limbs. The women and children were put on sale in the public market; the old men and boys driven with deadly bastonados to forced labour. Nor was this sufficient; in order to render indelible the stain on their criminal hands, the captors drove the people, after depriving them of their leaders and spokesmen, out of the towns at all hours of the day and night, half-naked, straight out of their beds; plundered their houses, burnt the villages, destroyed the churches or turned them into mosques, carried off the cattle, seized all the vehicles, snatched the bread out of the mouths of their victims, tore the clothes from off their backs, the gold from their hair. Officials—military officers, soldiers, shepherds—vied with one another in their wild orgy of blood, dragging out of the schools delicate orphan to serve their bestial lusts, beat with cudgels dying women or women close on childbirth who could scarcely drag themselves along, until the women fell down on the road and died, changing the dust beneath them into bloodstained mire. Travellers passing along the road turned away their eyes in horror from this moving multitude, driven on with devilish cruelty —only to find in their inns new-born babes buried in the dung-heaps of the court-yards, and the roads covered with severed heads of boys, who had raised them in supplication to their torturers. Parties which on their departure from the homeland of High Armenia consisted of thousands, numbered on their arrival in the outskirts of Aleppo only a few hundreds, while the fields were strewed with swollen, blackened corpses, infecting the air with their odours, lying about desecrated, naked, having been robbed of their clothes, or driven, bound back to back, to the Euphrates to provide food for the fishes. Sometimes gendarmes in derision threw into the emaciated hands of the starving people a little meal which they greedily licked off, merely with the result of prolonging their death-agony.

Even before the gates of Aleppo they were allowed no rest. For incomprehensible and utterly unjustifiable reasons of war, the shrunken parties were ceaselessly driven barefooted, hundreds of miles under a burning sun, through stony defiles, over pathless steppes, enfeebled by fever and other maladies, through semi-tropical marshes, into the wilderness of desolation. Here they died—slain by Kurds, robbed by gendarmes, shot, hanged, poisoned, stabbed, strangled, mown down by epidemics, drowned, frozen, parched with thirst, starved—their bodies left to putrefy or to be devoured by jackals.

Children wept themselves to death, men dashed themselves against the rocks, mothers threw their babes into the brooks, women with child flung themselves, singing, into the Euphrates. They died all the deaths on the earth, the deaths of all the,, ages.

I have seen maddened deportees eating as food their own clothes and shoes, women cooking the bodies of their new-born babes.

In ruined caravanserais they lay between heaps of corpses and half-rotted bodies, with no one to pity them, waiting for death; for how long would it be possible for them to drag out a miserable existence, searching out grains of corn from horse-dung or eating grass? But all this is only a fraction of what I have seen myself, of what I have been told by my acquaintances or by travellers, or of what I have heard from the mouths of the deportees.

Mr. President, if you will look through that dreadful enumeration of horrors compiled by Lord Bryce in England and by Dr. Johannes Lepsius in Germany with regard to these occurrences, you will see that I am not exaggerating. But I may assume that these pictures of horrors of which all the world has heard except Germany, which has been shamefully deceived, are already in your hands. By what right, then, do I make this appeal to you?

I do it by the right of human fellowship, in dutiful fulfilment of a sacred promise.

When in the desert I went through the deportees' camp, when I sat in their tents with the starving and dying, I felt their supplicating hands in mine, and the voices of their priests, who had blessed many of the dead on their last journey to the grave, adjured me to plead for them, if I were ever in Europe again.

But the country to which I have returned is a poor country; Germany is a conquered nation. My own people (the Germans) are near starvation; the streets are full of the poor and wretched. Can I beg help of a people which perhaps will soon not be in a condition to save itself for a people (the Armenians) which is in even more evil case?

The voice of conscience and humanity will never be silenced in me, and therefore I address these words to you.

This document is a request. It is the tongues of a thousand dead that speak in it.

Mr. President, the wrong suffered by this people is immeasurable. I have read everything that has been written about the war. I have carefully made myself acquainted with the horrors in every country on this earth, the fearful slaughters in every battle, the ships sunk by torpedoes, the bombs thrown down on the towns by air-craft, the heartrending slaughters in Belgium, the misery of the French refugees, the fearful sickness and epidemics in Roumania. But here is wrong to be righted such as none of these peoples has suffered—neither the French nation, nor the Belgian, nor the English, nor the Russian, nor the Serbian, nor the Roumanian, nor even the German nation, which has had to suffer so much in this war. The barbarous peoples of ancient times may possibly have endured a similar fate. But here we have a highly civilised nation, with a great and glorious past, which has rendered services that can never be forgotten to art, literature and learning; a nation which has produced many remarkable and intellectual men, profoundly religious, with a noble priesthood; a Christian people, whose members are dispersed over the whole earth, many of whom have lived for many years in your country, Mr. President. Men acquainted with all the languages of the world, men whose wives and daughters have been accustomed to sit in comfortable chairs at a table covered with a clean white cloth, not to crouch in a cave in the wilderness. Sagacious merchants, distinguished doctors, scholars, artists, honest prosperous peasants who made the land fruitful, and whose only fault was that they were defenceless and spoke a different language from that of their persecutors, and were born into a different faith.

Every one who knows the events of this war in Anatolia, who has followed the fortunes of this nation with open eyes, knows that all those accusations which were brought, with great cunning and much diligence, against the Armenian race, are nothing but loathsome slanders fabricated by their unscrupulous tyrants, in order to shield themselves from the consequences of their own mad and brutal acts, and to hide their own incapacity for reconciliation with the spirit of sincerity and humanity.

But even if all these accusations were based on the truth, they would never justify these cruel deeds committed against hundreds of thousands of innocent people.

I am making no accusation against Islam. The spirit of every great religion is noble, and the conduct of many a Mohammedan has made us blush for the deeds of Europe.

I do not accuse the simple people of Turkey, whose souls are full of goodness; but I do not think that the members of the ruling class will ever, in the course of history, be capable of making their country happy, for they have destroyed our belief in their capacity for civilisation.

Turkey has forfeited for all time the right to govern itself.

Mr. President, you will believe in my impartiality if I speak to you on this subject, as a German, one of a nation which was linked with Turkey in bonds of close friendship, a nation which in consequence of this friendship has most unjustly been accused of being an accomplice in these murderous man-hunts. The German people knows nothing of this crime. The German Government erred through ignorance of the Turkish character and its own preoccupation with solicitude for the future of its own people. I do not deny that weakness is a fault in the life of nations. But the bitter reproach of having made possible this unpardonable deportation does not fall on Germany alone.

In the Berlin Treaty of July 1878, all the six European Great Powers gave the most solemn guarantees that they would guard the tranquillity and security of the Armenian people. But has this promise ever been kept? Even Abdul Hamid's massacres failed to bring it to remembrance, and in blind greed the nations pursued selfish aims, not one putting itself forward as the champion of an oppressed people.

In the Armistice between Turkey and your Allies, which the Armenians all over the world awaited with feverish anxiety, the Armenian question is scarcely mentioned. Shall this unworthy game be repeated a second time, and must the Armenians be once more disillusioned?

The future of this small nation must not be relegated to obscurity behind the selfish schemes and plans of the great states. Mr. President, save the honour of Europe.

It would be an irremediable mistake if the Armenian districts of Russia were not joined with the Armenian provinces of Anatolia and Cilicia to form one common country entirely liberated from Turkish rule, with an outlet of its own to the sea. It is not enough, Mr. President, that you should know the sufferings of these people. It is not enough that you should give them a state in which the houses are destroyed, the fields laid waste, the citizens murdered. The exhaustion of this country is such that by its own strength it cannot rise again. Its trade is ruined; its handicrafts and industries have collapsed. The asset of its annihilated population can never be restored.

Many thousands of Armenians were perverted to Islam by force, thousands of children and girls kidnapped, and thousands of women carried away and made slaves in Turkish harems. To all these must be given perfect assurance of their return to freedom. All victims of persecution who are returning to their homes after spending two years and more in the desert must be indemnified for the wealth and goods that they have lost, all orphans must be cared for. What these people need is love, of which they have so long been deprived. This is, for all of us, a confession of guilt.

Mr. President, pride prevents me from pleading for my own people (the Germans). I have no doubt that, out of the plenitude of its sorrow, it will gain power by sacrifice to co-operate in the future redemption of the world. But, on behalf of the Armenian nation, which has suffered such terrible tyranny, I venture to intervene; for if, after this war, it is not given reparation for its fearful sufferings, it will be lost for ever.

With the ardour of one who has experienced unspeakable, humiliating sorrows in his own tortured soul, I utter the voice of those unhappy ones, whose despairing cries I had to hear without being able to still them, whose cruel deaths I could only helplessly mourn, whose bones bestrew the deserts of the Euphrates, and whose limbs once more become alive in my heart and admonish me to speak.

Once already have I knocked at the door of the American people when I brought the petition of the deportees from their camps at Meskene and Aleppo to your Embassy at Constantinople, and I know that this has not been in vain.

If you, Mr. President, have indeed made the sublime idea of championing oppressed nations the guiding principle of your policy, you will not fail to perceive that even in these words a mighty voice speaks, the only voice that has the right to be heard at all times—the voice of humanity.

Appendix II

The following images were originally embedded in Naim Bey's 1920 text, but in this edition are all here placed at the end.

Appendix III has 26 additional images which were not included, but rather accompanied the 1964 reprint commemorating the fiftieth anniversary of the genocide.

Converted Armenian orphans in the orphanage at Beyrut, and the Turkish staff, imparting Turkish education to these orphans

Halide Hanum (sitting), a Turkish authoress, a most active worker at the conversion of Armenian orphans to Islam. An Armenian girl (standing) is being allured into harem life

Djemal Pasha (x), followed by his aide-de-camp, Nusret Bey, and Hassan Bey, the Director of Deportations, reviewing the Armenian orphans at Damascus

Armenian orphans picked up in the desert

Halide Hanum, accompanied by converted Armenian orphans

Hakki Bey, commissioned to direct the massacres
of straggling Armenians in the desert

Armenian women refugees devouring the flesh of dead horses

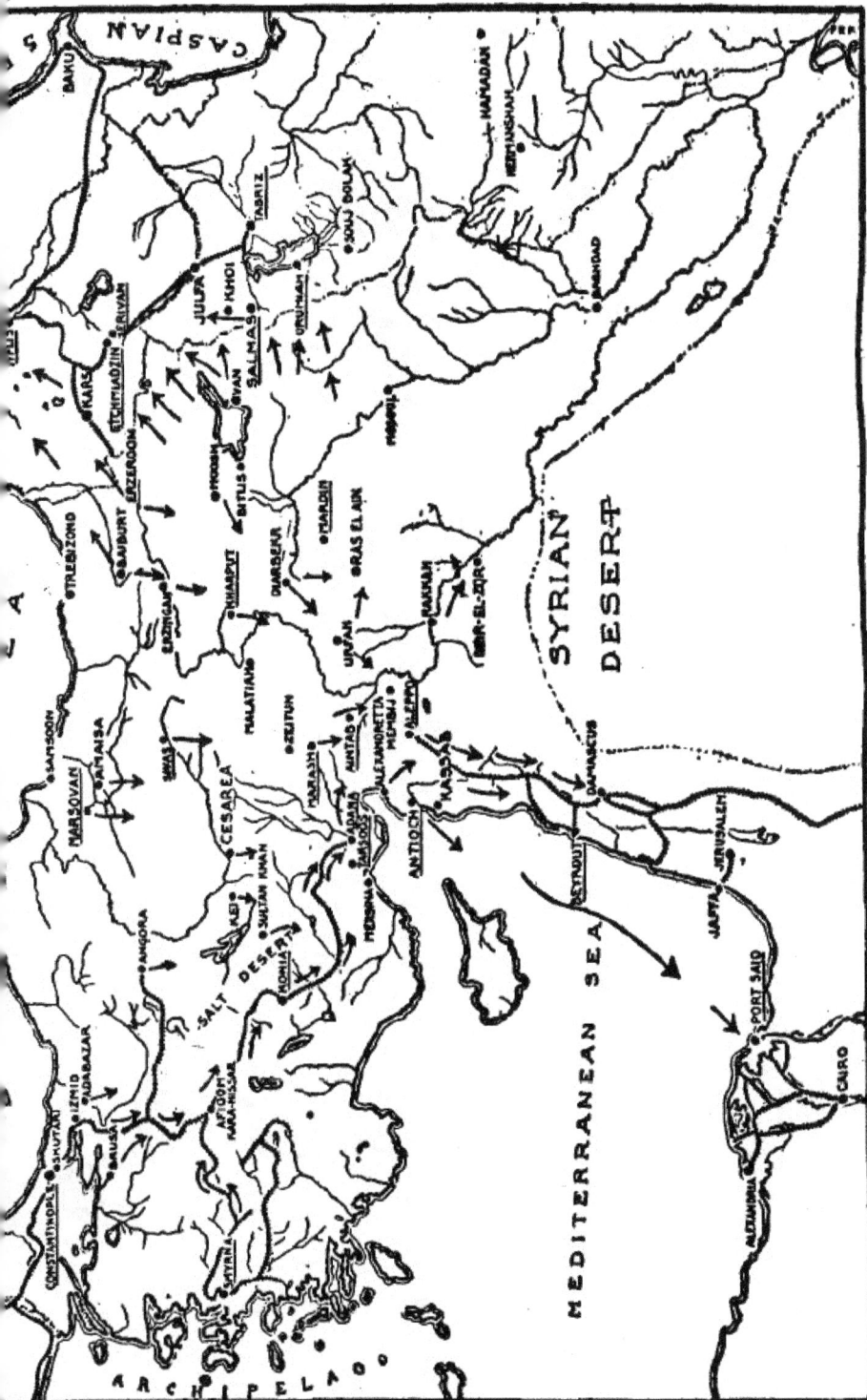

Arrows Showing Origins and Directions of Mass Deportations.

(continued on next page)

No. 2.

No. 3.

No. 4.

ه.

دخيليه نظارهٔ جليله سنه يكٖ وربنجه شعبهٔ ثانيه نامج و ٨٥٤
نمروله مشروح نفقرهنك نند صورتيدر.

مختوجه جيوب دنلگ بشكمه صاحطلي جيوه ولشزن اسمه انباع ولشمه
ومجود آتيلهه آننك نه مقصدله نه نفع بيكله قوليم اثره محلله اولاده
ريانجي اولان وصيله ونزكاً خصوصيه سنه استثنا وامجوزه معاهدناك
اظهار يي موافق ديسنه . . . بوكيبدن صرفيان قطع ليه زريفنده ولاه
وكمهد وفه . . . اهد آيلهكه ، اراهلدن وصنيفنك يكره ومحمحه بزياولدر.

د نفيه نأولمس

يكاجهد مدر برادى مصدر نك طفنك

وطا
منطقه قباى

70

The following photos were not included in the original text, but were appended to the 1965 reprint, with a note stating as much by M. G. Sevag, Ph.D.

1. Women and Children Driven to an Unknown Destination

VIA DOLOROSA.

—Kirby in the New York *World*.

2. Via Dolorosa

3. After Slaughter

Turkish Brutality in Armenia—Հայաստան Թուրքերin
1916

4. After Slaughter

5. Parents murdered. A boy from Tokat tails the caravan of deportees.

6. Severed heads mounted on sticks. A Turkish festival of murder.
(Photographed by a German Officer in Turkey)

7. Turkish hangmen and their victims. *(A scene in a public square in Aleppo, 1915)*

8. Last days of starving children. (*Arabian Desert. Photograph by a German Officer in Turkey.*)

9. A starved Armenian mother with her two starved children.
(Arabian Desert. Photograph by a Vienese Officer in Turkey, 1916.)

10. A group of starved women and children. A monument for the glorification of Turkish Racism.
(*Photograph by a Viennese Officer, 1916.*)

11. Remains of mass murder by Turks *(Photograph by Miss Jacobson)*

12. After slaughter, in the Province of Ankara, Turkey.

13. **Turkish—German Fraternity.** *Turkish and German Officers celebrated the deportation of Erzuroum Armenians with wine and topped it with the raping of Armenian maidens.*

14. In the desert of Der-el-Zor. Why there are no living Armenians in the Armenian provinces in Turkey.

15. A scene of mass murder. (*Mesopotamia, 1915. Photograph by a German Officer in Turkey.*)

16. Hanged Armenian Doctors and the Turkish Hangmen.
   (Armenian physicians murdered by Turks, 60, and 41 died in Turkish Military Service of spotted typhus; pharmacists murdered, 31, and 15 died in military service of spotted typhus; dentists murdered, 8; Armenian medical students murdered, 13.)

17. A Mound of Skulls *of the murdered and starved Armenians in Der—el—zor gathered from the desert at the end of World War I.*

18. A public square of Erzinjan in Turkey. *An Armenian Theatre had been planned for this square, now the remains of the murdered Armenians act the roles of their tragedy.*

19. A quarry of skulls and bones of Armenians murdered by Turks.

20. The Turkish hangmen and Arab victims.

21. The parade of victims and their Turkish hangmen.

22. The Turkish hangmen and the Armenian victim whose battered face was hidden from view.

23. The parade of victims and their Turkish hangmen.

24. The parade of victims and their Turkish hangmen.

25. The Turkish hangman and the Armenian victims.

26. The exhibition of the heads of two Armenian clergymen and their Turkish assassins *(Photograph by a German Officer in Turkey).*

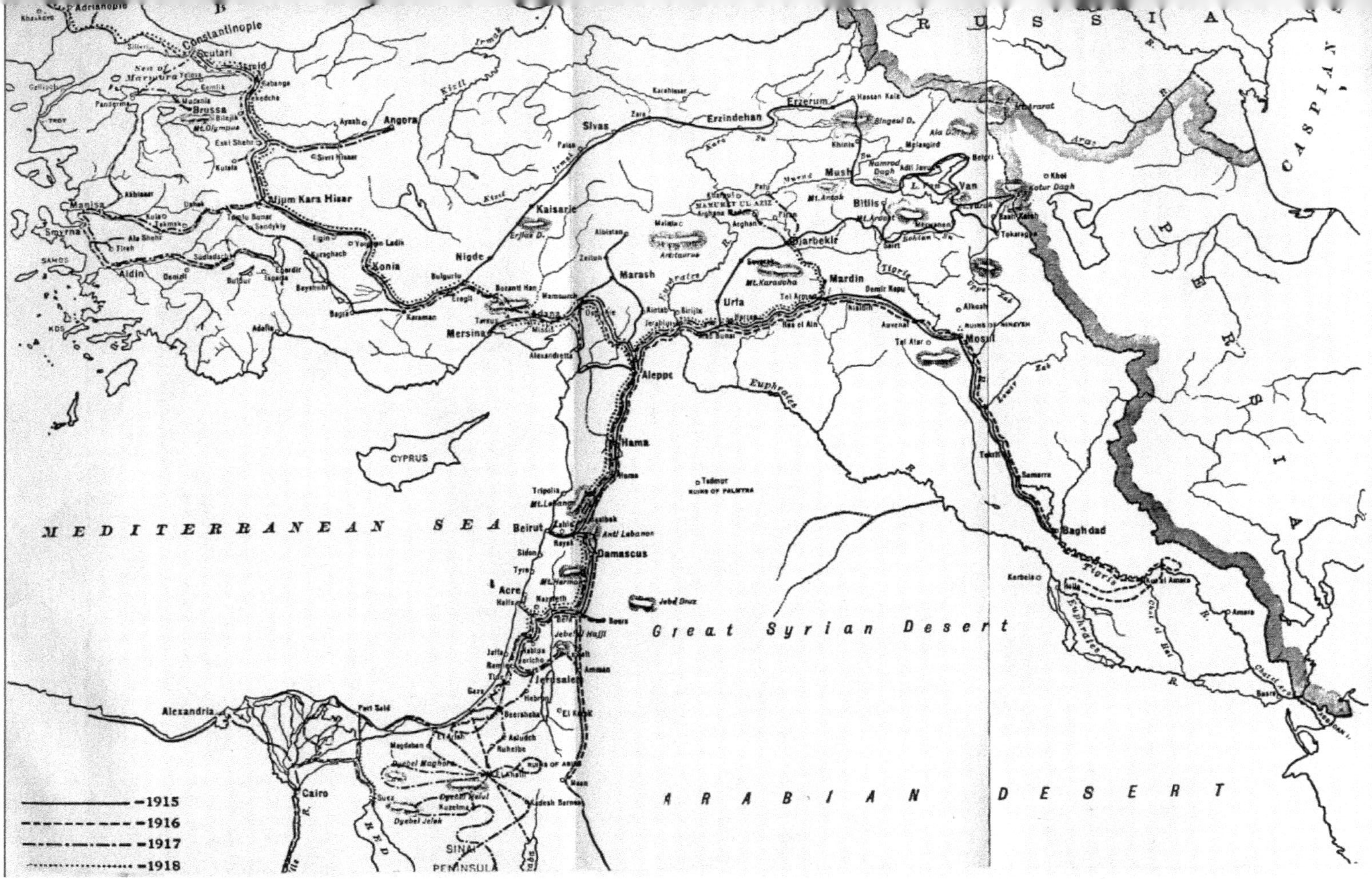
RUSSIA
CASPIAN
PERSIA
MEDITERRANEAN SEA
Great Syrian Desert
ARABIAN DESERT
CYPRUS
SINAI PENINSULA
Adrianople
Constantinople
Scutari
Ismid
Sea of Marmara
Brussa
Mt. Olympus
Eski Shehr
Angora
Sivas
Erzerum
Erzindehan
Mush
Bitlis
Van
Kaisarie
Nigde
Konia
Afium Kars Hisar
Manisa
Smyrna
Aidin
SAMOS
KOS
Adana
Mersina
Tarsus
Alexandretta
Marash
Aleppo
Urfa
Mardin
Diarbekir
Mosul
Hama
Homs
Tripolis
Beirut
Damascus
Sidon
Tyre
Acre
Haifa
Jaffa
Jerusalem
Amman
Gaza
Beersheba
Port Said
Alexandria
Cairo
Suez
Baghdad
Samarra
Kerbela
Euphrates
Tigris
Basra
Amara
Mt. Ararat
Tadmor
RUINS OF PALMYRA
Jebel Druz
—1915
-------1916
—·—·—1917
··········1918